DYLAN FOX

Django 5.1.x For Web Development

Copyright © 2024 by Dylan Fox

All rights reserved. No part of this publication may be reproduced, stored or transmitted in any form or by any means, electronic, mechanical, photocopying, recording, scanning, or otherwise without written permission from the publisher. It is illegal to copy this book, post it to a website, or distribute it by any other means without permission.

First edition

This book was professionally typeset on Reedsy. Find out more at reedsy.com

Contents

Introduction to Django	1
Chapter 1: Getting Started with Django	9
Chapter 2: Django Fundamentals	18
Chapter 3: Models and Databases	26
Chapter 4: Building User Interfaces	34
Chapter 5: User Authentication and Authorization	45
Chapter 6: Advanced Django Features	57
Chapter 7: RESTful APIs with Django	66
Chapter 8: Deployment and Maintenance	75
Chapter 9: Testing in Django	82
Chapter 10: Best Practices and Patterns	91
Conclusion	102

Scripting (XSS), Cross-Site Request Forgery (CSRF), and SQL Injection.
4. **Scalability**: Django is highly scalable, making it suitable for projects of any size. Whether you're building a small application or a large enterprise solution, Django can handle increasing traffic and data volumes efficiently.
5. **Modular Architecture**: Django follows a modular design, allowing developers to create reusable components. This promotes code reuse and helps in maintaining a clean project structure.
6. **Support for Multiple Databases**: Django supports various databases, including PostgreSQL, MySQL, SQLite, and Oracle. This flexibility allows developers to choose the database that best fits their project's requirements.
7. **Rich Ecosystem**: The Django ecosystem includes numerous third-party packages and libraries that extend its functionality. From authentication and payment processing to RESTful APIs, there is a wealth of resources available for developers.
8. **Community Support**: Django has a vibrant and active community of developers who contribute to its ongoing development and provide support through forums, documentation, and tutorials.

Getting Started with Django

To get started with Django, you'll need to install Python on your system, as Django is a Python-based framework. The installation process is straightforward:

1. **Install Python**: Download the latest version of Python from the official website and follow the installation instructions for your operating system.
2. **Install Django**: Use pip, Python's package manager, to install Django. You can do this by running the following command in your terminal:

bash

```
pip install django
```

1. **Create a New Project**: Once Django is installed, you can create a new project using the command:

bash

```
django-admin startproject projectname
```

1. This will create a new directory with the necessary files and folders for your Django project.
2. **Run the Development Server**: Navigate to your project directory and run the development server with the command:

bash

```
python manage.py runserver
```

1. You can then access your application in your web browser at http://127.0.0.1:8000/.

Conclusion

Django is a powerful and versatile framework that simplifies web development while promoting best practices and clean code. Its robust features, strong security measures, and active community make it an ideal choice for

Introduction to Django

Overview of Django

Django is a high-level Python web framework that encourages rapid development and clean, pragmatic design. It was created to simplify the complexities of web development, allowing developers to focus on writing their applications instead of dealing with repetitive tasks. Since its inception in 2005, Django has gained immense popularity among developers due to its flexibility, scalability, and robust features.

At its core, Django follows the **Model-View-Template (MVT)** architectural pattern. This design pattern separates the data model, user interface, and control logic, promoting clean and maintainable code. Each component serves a distinct role:

- **Model**: Represents the data structure and business logic. It defines the database schema and interacts with the database.
- **View**: Handles the logic behind processing user requests and returns the appropriate responses. Views are where the business logic resides.
- **Template**: Manages the presentation layer. Templates define how the data is presented to the user, typically in HTML format.

Django's primary goal is to ease the development of complex, database-driven websites. It provides developers with a robust set of tools and libraries, enabling them to build applications efficiently and with fewer errors.

History of Django

Django was created by Adrian Holovaty and Simon Willison in 2003 while working at the Lawrence Journal-World newspaper. They aimed to create a web framework that would facilitate the rapid development of web applications, particularly for managing content. The framework was named after the famous jazz guitarist Django Reinhardt, reflecting its emphasis on creativity and elegance.

In 2005, Django was released as an open-source project, allowing developers worldwide to contribute and enhance its capabilities. Over the years, Django has evolved significantly, with numerous versions released, each introducing new features and improvements. The latest major version, Django 5.1.x, builds upon the framework's strengths while incorporating modern web development practices.

Key Features of Django

Django boasts a wide array of features that make it a preferred choice for web development:

1. **Built-in Admin Interface**: Django comes with a powerful admin panel that enables developers to manage the application's data effortlessly. This interface is automatically generated from the defined models, providing a convenient way to perform CRUD operations.
2. **Robust ORM (Object-Relational Mapping)**: Django's ORM allows developers to interact with the database using Python objects instead of writing SQL queries. This abstraction simplifies database operations and enhances code readability.
3. **Security**: Django is designed with security in mind. It provides built-in protections against common web vulnerabilities, such as Cross-Site

developers looking to build dynamic web applications quickly. As we delve deeper into the subsequent chapters, we will explore Django's components, features, and best practices, equipping you with the knowledge and skills to create successful web applications using Django.

Why Choose Django for Web Development?

1. Rapid Development

One of the most compelling reasons to choose Django for web development is its emphasis on rapid development. The framework is designed to help developers build applications quickly and efficiently. Here's how Django facilitates rapid development:

- **Built-in Admin Interface**: As mentioned earlier, Django's automatic admin interface allows developers to manage the application's data without having to create separate interfaces manually. This feature significantly speeds up the development process.
- **Code Reusability**: Django's modular architecture encourages code reuse. Developers can create reusable components and applications, reducing the amount of code needed for new projects.
- **Comprehensive Documentation**: Django boasts extensive documentation that covers every aspect of the framework. This resource allows developers to quickly find the information they need, reducing the time spent on troubleshooting and implementation.

2. Security Features

Web applications are often targeted by malicious users and hackers. Django recognizes this threat and provides several built-in security features to protect your application:

- **Protection Against Common Vulnerabilities**: Django includes pro-

tections against SQL injection, Cross-Site Scripting (XSS), Cross-Site Request Forgery (CSRF), and clickjacking. These features are enabled by default, making it easier for developers to build secure applications.
- **User Authentication**: Django's built-in authentication system simplifies user management, allowing developers to implement secure user registration, login, and password management.
- **Secure Password Storage**: Django uses password hashing to store user passwords securely. This ensures that even if a hacker gains access to the database, they cannot easily retrieve user passwords.

3. Scalability

Django is highly scalable, making it suitable for projects of any size, from small applications to large-scale enterprise solutions. Key aspects of Django's scalability include:

- **Efficient ORM**: Django's Object-Relational Mapping (ORM) allows developers to interact with the database using Python objects, making it easier to optimize queries and manage large datasets.
- **Support for Multiple Databases**: Django can work with various databases, allowing developers to choose the one that best fits their scalability requirements.
- **Horizontal Scaling**: Django applications can be deployed across multiple servers to handle increased traffic, ensuring that the application remains responsive and performant.

4. Versatility

Django is a versatile framework that can be used to build a wide range of web applications. Whether you're creating a simple blog, an e-commerce platform, or a complex social network, Django has the tools and features to support your project:

- **Support for RESTful APIs**: With the Django REST Framework, developers can easily create RESTful APIs that enable communication between different parts of the application or with third-party services.
- **Integration with Frontend Frameworks**: Django can be used alongside popular frontend frameworks such as React, Angular, and Vue.js, allowing developers to create dynamic, interactive user interfaces.
- **Content Management Systems**: Many popular content management systems, such as Wagtail and Django CMS, are built on Django, demonstrating its capabilities in managing content-driven websites.

5. Community and Ecosystem

Django has a vibrant community of developers who contribute to its ongoing development and support:

- **Active Community**: The Django community is known for its friendliness and willingness to help newcomers. Developers can find assistance through forums, Stack Overflow, and various online resources.
- **Third-Party Packages**: The Django ecosystem includes numerous third-party packages that extend its functionality. From authentication and payment processing to data visualization and analytics, developers can find libraries that meet their specific needs.
- **Regular Updates**: Django receives regular updates, ensuring that the framework remains relevant and continues to support modern web development practices.

6. Robust Testing Framework

Testing is an essential part of the development process, and Django provides a robust testing framework that makes it easy to write and run tests:

- **Built-in Testing Tools**: Django includes built-in tools for creating unit tests, integration tests, and functional tests. This allows developers to

ensure that their applications are reliable and bug-free.
- **Test Automation**: Django's testing framework supports automation, enabling developers to run tests automatically as part of their deployment process. This helps maintain code quality and stability.

7. Good Documentation

Django is known for its comprehensive and well-structured documentation. This resource is invaluable for both beginners and experienced developers:

- **Getting Started Guides**: Django's documentation includes clear getting started guides that help new developers set up their environment and build their first application quickly.
- **API Reference**: The API reference provides detailed information about every aspect of the framework, including models, views, templates, and more.
- **Best Practices**: The documentation also covers best practices for building Django applications, ensuring that developers are aware of the recommended approaches.

Conclusion

Choosing Django for web development offers numerous advantages, including rapid development, robust security, scalability, and a vibrant community. Its versatility allows developers to create a wide range of applications, while its comprehensive documentation makes it accessible to newcomers and experienced developers alike. Whether you're building a simple blog or a complex e-commerce platform, Django provides the tools and features needed to succeed in today's competitive web development landscape.

Chapter 1: Getting Started with Django

Django is a powerful web framework that simplifies the development process of dynamic websites. This chapter will guide you through the initial steps of setting up Django, from installation to creating your first project. By the end, you'll have a solid foundation to build your web applications.

1.1 Overview of Django

Django is a high-level Python web framework that enables rapid development and promotes clean, pragmatic design. It was designed to help developers create complex web applications quickly and efficiently, focusing on the principles of reusability and the "Don't Repeat Yourself" (DRY) philosophy. Here are some key features of Django that make it an appealing choice for web development:

- **MVT Architecture**: Django follows the Model-View-Template (MVT) architectural pattern, which separates data handling (model), business logic (view), and presentation (template).
- **Robust ORM**: Django's Object-Relational Mapping (ORM) allows developers to interact with databases using Python objects rather than writing complex SQL queries, streamlining database operations.
- **Security Features**: Django includes several built-in security features

to protect web applications from common threats like SQL injection, Cross-Site Scripting (XSS), and Cross-Site Request Forgery (CSRF).
- **Rich Ecosystem**: The Django ecosystem boasts numerous third-party packages and libraries that enhance functionality and provide additional features for developers.
- **Scalability**: Django is suitable for projects of all sizes, making it easy to scale applications as traffic increases.
- **Active Community**: With a large community of developers, Django benefits from ongoing contributions, updates, and support.

This chapter will provide a step-by-step guide to getting started with Django, ensuring that you have a solid foundation for your web development journey.

1.2 Setting Up the Development Environment

Before you can begin working with Django, you need to set up your development environment. This involves installing Python, Django, and a virtual environment to manage dependencies.

1.2.1 Installing Python

Django is built on Python, so the first step is to install Python on your system. Here's how to do it:

Windows

1. **Download Python**: Visit the official Python website and download the latest version of Python. Be sure to choose the appropriate installer for your operating system.
2. **Run the Installer**: Double-click the downloaded file to run the installer. During installation, make sure to check the box that says "Add Python to PATH."
3. **Verify Installation**: Open the Command Prompt and type the following command to verify that Python is installed correctly:

CHAPTER 1: GETTING STARTED WITH DJANGO

```bash
python --version
```

1. You should see the version of Python that you installed.

macOS

1. **Install Homebrew** (if not already installed): Open the Terminal and run the following command to install Homebrew, a package manager for macOS:

```bash
/bin/bash -c "$(curl -fsSL https://raw.githubusercontent.com/Homebrew/install/HEAD/install.sh)"
```

1. **Install Python**: Use Homebrew to install Python by running:

```bash
brew install python
```

1. **Verify Installation**: Check that Python is installed correctly:

bash

```
python3 --version
```

Linux

1. **Install Python**: Most Linux distributions come with Python pre-installed. To check if Python is installed, open the Terminal and run:

bash

```
python3 --version
```

1. If Python is not installed, you can install it using the package manager for your distribution. For example, on Ubuntu, run:

bash

```
sudo apt update
sudo apt install python3
```

1.2.2 Installing Django

Once Python is installed, you can proceed to install Django. It's recommended to install Django using pip, Python's package manager.

1. **Open the Terminal or Command Prompt**: Depending on your operating system, open the command line interface.
2. **Install Django**: Run the following command to install the latest version of Django:

```bash
pip install django
```

1. **Verify Installation**: After the installation is complete, verify that Django is installed correctly by checking its version:

```bash
python -m django --version
```

1. This command should return the version of Django you installed.

1.2.3 Setting Up a Virtual Environment

Using a virtual environment is essential for managing dependencies and isolating projects. It allows you to create a separate environment for each Django project, preventing conflicts between packages.

Creating a Virtual Environment

1. **Navigate to Your Project Directory**: Use the Terminal or Command Prompt to navigate to the directory where you want to create your Django project.

```bash
cd path/to/your/project-directory
```

1. **Create a Virtual Environment**: Run the following command to create a new virtual environment named venv:

```bash
python -m venv venv
```

1. This will create a new directory named venv in your project directory.

Activating the Virtual Environment

- **Windows**:

```bash
venv\Scripts\activate
```

- **macOS and Linux**:

```bash
source venv/bin/activate
```

Once activated, your command line prompt will change, indicating that you are now working within the virtual environment. You can now install Django and any other packages without affecting your system-wide Python installation.

1.3 Creating Your First Django Project

Now that you have set up your development environment, it's time to create your first Django project.

1.3.1 Project Structure

To create a new Django project, you'll use the django-admin command-line tool.

1. **Create a New Django Project**: Run the following command, replacing myproject with your desired project name:

```bash
django-admin startproject myproject
```

1. This command will create a new directory named myproject containing the following structure:

```markdown
myproject/
    manage.py
    myproject/
        __init__.py
        settings.py
        urls.py
        wsgi.py
```

- **manage.py**: A command-line utility that allows you to interact with your

Django project. You can run the development server, apply migrations, and more using this file.
- **settings.py**: Contains all the configuration settings for your project, including database settings, installed apps, middleware, and more.
- **urls.py**: Defines the URL patterns for your project. This file maps URLs to views, allowing you to specify which views should be executed for different requests.
- **wsgi.py**: A file for deploying your application to a web server. It serves as the entry point for WSGI-compatible web servers to run your Django application.

1.3.2 Running the Development Server

With your project created, you can now run the Django development server to see your project in action.

1. **Navigate to Your Project Directory**: Change to the project directory:

```bash
cd myproject
```

1. **Run the Development Server**: Start the development server with the following command:

```bash
python manage.py runserver
```

1. You should see output indicating that the server is running, similar to the following:

```arduino
Starting development server at http://127.0.0.1:8000/
```

1. **Access Your Application**: Open your web browser and navigate to http://127.0.0.1:8000/. You should see a welcome screen indicating that your Django project is set up and running.

Conclusion

In this chapter, you learned how to set up your development environment for Django, install Python and Django, create a virtual environment, and create your first Django project. With this foundation, you're now ready to explore the powerful features and capabilities of Django as you continue your web development journey. In the following chapters, we will dive deeper into Django's components, including models, views, and templates, as well as best practices for building robust web applications.

Chapter 2: Django Fundamentals

Django is built around the principles of the Model-View-Template (MVT) architecture, which is an adaptation of the Model-View-Controller (MVC) design pattern commonly used in web applications. This chapter will provide an in-depth understanding of Django's architecture, how to structure your project using apps, and how to define URL patterns and views to handle user requests.

2.1 Understanding the MVC Pattern

While Django follows the MVT pattern, it's essential to understand the MVC concept as it forms the foundation of Django's design.

The MVC Pattern

The MVC pattern separates an application into three interconnected components:

- **Model**: Represents the data and the business logic of the application. It interacts with the database and defines how data is stored and retrieved. In Django, models are defined as Python classes that map to database tables.
- **View**: Handles the user interface and user interaction. Views retrieve

data from the model and render it for display. In Django, views are functions or classes that process requests and return responses.
- **Controller**: Manages the communication between the model and the view. It responds to user input and interacts with the model to update the view. In Django, the URL dispatcher acts as the controller, directing incoming requests to the appropriate view based on the requested URL.

Django's MVT Pattern

Django's adaptation of MVC, known as MVT, has a few notable differences:

- **Model**: Remains the same as in MVC. In Django, you define models in the models.py file of an app.
- **View**: In Django, views serve as the intermediary between the model and the template. They fetch data from the model and pass it to the template for rendering.
- **Template**: Instead of a controller, Django uses templates to handle the presentation layer. Templates are HTML files that define how data is presented to the user.

The MVT architecture allows for a clean separation of concerns, making it easier to maintain and extend your application.

2.2 Django Apps: Structuring Your Project

Django encourages a modular approach to application development through the use of apps. An app is a self-contained package that encapsulates a specific piece of functionality within your project.

Creating a Django App

To create a new app, you can use the startapp command. Here's how to do it:

1. **Navigate to Your Project Directory**: Open your terminal or command prompt and navigate to your Django project directory.

```bash
cd myproject
```

1. **Create a New App**: Run the following command, replacing myapp with the desired name for your app:

```bash
python manage.py startapp myapp
```

This command creates a new directory named myapp containing the following structure:

```markdown
myapp/
    migrations/
        __init__.py
    __init__.py
    admin.py
    apps.py
    models.py
    tests.py
```

```
views.py
```

- **migrations/**: Contains files for database migrations related to this app.
- **admin.py**: Used to register models for the Django admin interface.
- **apps.py**: Contains application configuration settings.
- **models.py**: Defines the data models for the app.
- **tests.py**: Contains tests for the app.
- **views.py**: Defines the views that handle user requests.

Organizing Your Project

As your project grows, you'll likely have multiple apps. Here are some best practices for organizing your Django project:

1. **One App per Feature**: Each app should focus on a specific feature or functionality. For example, if you're building an e-commerce site, you might have separate apps for products, orders, and users.
2. **Reusability**: Design your apps to be reusable. If you create a generic app that can be used in multiple projects, you can save time in future development.
3. **Follow Naming Conventions**: Use lowercase, descriptive names for your apps (e.g., blog, shop). This helps maintain clarity and consistency throughout your project.
4. **Use a Consistent Structure**: Each app should follow a consistent directory structure to make it easier to navigate and understand.

2.3 URL Routing and Views

In Django, URL routing and views work together to handle incoming requests. The URL dispatcher maps URLs to corresponding views, allowing you to define how your application responds to different requests.

2.3.1 Defining URL Patterns

Django uses URL patterns to determine which view should handle a specific request. URL patterns are defined in the urls.py file of your app or project.
   Creating a urls.py File

1. **Create urls.py**: If it doesn't already exist, create a new file named urls.py in your app directory (myapp/urls.py).
2. **Import Required Modules**: In urls.py, import the necessary modules and functions:

```python
from django.urls import path
from . import views
```

1. **Define URL Patterns**: Create a list of URL patterns, mapping URLs to views:

```python
urlpatterns = [
    path('', views.home, name='home'),
    path('about/', views.about, name='about'),
]
```

In this example, the home view will handle requests to the root URL, while the about view will handle requests to /about/.
   Including App URLs in Project URLs
   To connect your app's URLs to the main project's URL configuration, you need to modify the urls.py file in your project directory (myproject/urls.py):

1. **Import Include**: Add the import statement for include:

```python
from django.urls import path, include
```

1. **Include App URLs**: Modify the urlpatterns list to include the app's URLs:

```python
urlpatterns = [
    path('', include('myapp.urls')),
]
```

This setup allows Django to route requests to your app's URL patterns.

2.3.2 Creating Views

Views in Django handle the logic for processing requests and returning responses. Views can be defined as functions or classes, depending on the complexity of your application.

Creating Function-Based Views

To create a simple function-based view:

1. **Open views.py**: Navigate to your app's views.py file.
2. **Define a View Function**: Create a view function that takes a request and returns a response:

```python
from django.http import HttpResponse

def home(request):
    return HttpResponse("Welcome to the Home Page!")

def about(request):
    return HttpResponse("This is the About Page.")
```

In this example, the home view returns a simple welcome message, while the about view provides a description of the about page.

Creating Class-Based Views

Django also supports class-based views, which provide more structure and can handle multiple HTTP methods.

To create a class-based view:

1. **Import Required Modules**: In views.py, import the necessary classes:

```python
from django.views import View
from django.http import HttpResponse
```

1. **Define a Class-Based View**:

```python
class HomeView(View):
    def get(self, request):
        return HttpResponse("Welcome to the Home Page!")
```

1. **Update URL Patterns**: Modify your urls.py to use the class-based view:

```python
urlpatterns = [
    path('', HomeView.as_view(), name='home'),
]
```

Conclusion

In this chapter, you learned the fundamentals of Django, including the MVC pattern, how to structure your project with apps, and how to define URL patterns and views. Understanding these concepts is crucial for building robust and maintainable web applications with Django. In the next chapters, we will dive deeper into models, templates, and other advanced features of the Django framework.

Chapter 3: Models and Databases

In Django, models serve as the backbone of your application's data structure. They define how data is stored, retrieved, and manipulated within the application. This chapter will guide you through the essentials of Django models, database configuration, and querying your database effectively.

3.1 Introduction to Django Models

Django models are Python classes that represent your application's data structure. Each model class corresponds to a database table, and each instance of a model represents a row in that table. Django's Object-Relational Mapping (ORM) allows developers to interact with the database using Python objects, simplifying data manipulation and retrieval.

Key Features of Django Models

- **Field Types**: Django provides various field types (e.g., CharField, IntegerField, DateField) that map to corresponding database column types.
- **Validation**: Models come with built-in validation, ensuring that the data meets specific requirements before it is saved to the database.
- **Relationships**: Models can define relationships between each other

using fields such as ForeignKey, ManyToManyField, and OneToOneField.

- **Meta Options**: Models can include metadata, such as the ordering of records, unique constraints, and verbose names, to customize their behavior.

Defining a Model

To define a model, you typically create a class in the models.py file of your app. Here's an example of a simple model for a blog application:

```python
from django.db import models

class Post(models.Model):
    title = models.CharField(max_length=200)
    content = models.TextField()
    created_at = models.DateTimeField(auto_now_add=True)
    updated_at = models.DateTimeField(auto_now=True)

    def __str__(self):
        return self.title
```

In this example, the Post model has four fields: title, content, created_at, and updated_at. The __str__ method provides a readable string representation of the model instance.

3.2 Database Configuration

Before you can use Django models, you need to configure your database settings. Django supports several database backends, allowing you to choose the one that best fits your needs.

3.2.1 Supported Databases

Django natively supports several databases, including:

- **SQLite**: The default database engine for Django, which is lightweight and easy to set up. Suitable for development and small projects.
- **PostgreSQL**: A powerful, open-source relational database known for its robustness and performance. Recommended for production applications.
- **MySQL**: A widely used relational database that is suitable for various applications, especially those requiring high read/write performance.
- **Oracle**: An enterprise-level database system that provides advanced features for large applications.

Django can also work with other databases through third-party packages.

3.2.2 Configuring Database Settings

Django's database settings are configured in the settings.py file of your project. Here's how to configure your database:

1. **Open settings.py**: Navigate to your project directory and open the settings.py file.
2. **Locate the DATABASES Setting**: By default, Django uses SQLite. Modify the DATABASES setting to configure your desired database engine. Here's an example configuration for PostgreSQL:

```python
DATABASES = {
    'default': {
        'ENGINE': 'django.db.backends.postgresql',
        'NAME': 'mydatabase',
```

```
        'USER': 'myuser',
        'PASSWORD': 'mypassword',
        'HOST': 'localhost',
        'PORT': '5432',
    }
}
```

In this example, you need to replace mydatabase, myuser, and mypassword with your actual database name, username, and password.

3.3 Creating and Migrating Models

Once you have defined your models, you need to create database tables that correspond to those models. This process involves creating migrations and applying them to your database.

3.3.1 Model Fields and Types

Django provides various field types for different data types. Here are some commonly used field types:

- **CharField**: A string field for small to medium-sized text. Requires a max_length attribute.
- **TextField**: A field for larger text content. Does not require a max_length.
- **IntegerField**: A field for storing integer values.
- **DateTimeField**: A field for storing date and time information.
- **ForeignKey**: A field for establishing a many-to-one relationship with another model.
- **ManyToManyField**: A field for establishing a many-to-many relationship with another model.

Here's an example of defining fields in a model:

python

```
class Comment(models.Model):
    post = models.ForeignKey(Post, on_delete=models.CASCADE)
    author = models.CharField(max_length=100)
    content = models.TextField()
    created_at = models.DateTimeField(auto_now_add=True)
```

In this example, the Comment model has a foreign key relationship with the Post model, linking each comment to a specific post.

3.3.2 Running Migrations

After defining your models, you need to create and apply migrations to reflect the changes in the database.

Creating Migrations

To create migrations for your models, run the following command in your terminal:

bash

```
python manage.py makemigrations
```

This command will generate migration files that describe the changes to be made to the database.

Applying Migrations

To apply the migrations and create the corresponding tables in the database, run:

bash

```
python manage.py migrate
```

This command will execute the migration files and create or update the database schema accordingly.

3.4 Querying the Database

Once your models are set up and migrations have been applied, you can start querying the database using Django's ORM.

3.4.1 ORM Basics

Django's ORM allows you to interact with the database using Python objects, providing a high-level abstraction for database operations. Here are some basic operations you can perform using the ORM:

- **Creating Objects**: To create a new instance of a model, you can use the create() method or instantiate the model directly and call save():

```python
# Using create()
post = Post.objects.create(title='My
First Post', content='This is the content of my first post.')

# Using save()
post = Post(title='My Second Post',
  content='This is the content of my second post.')
post.save()
```

- **Retrieving Objects**: To retrieve objects from the database, you can use methods such as all(), get(), and filter():

```python
# Retrieve all posts
posts = Post.objects.all()

# Get a single post by ID
post = Post.objects.get(id=1)

# Filter posts by title
filtered_posts = Post.objects.
filter(title__icontains='first')
```

3.4.2 Filtering and Aggregation

Django's ORM also supports filtering and aggregation, allowing you to perform complex queries with ease.

Filtering

You can filter query results using various lookups. Here are some examples:

- **Exact Match**: Post.objects.filter(title='My First Post')
- **Case-Insensitive Match**: Post.objects.filter(title__iexact='my first post')
- **Contains**: Post.objects.filter(content__contains='content')
- **Date Filtering**: Post.objects.filter(created_at__year=2024)

You can chain multiple filters together to narrow down your results:

```python
recent_posts = Post.objects.
filter(created_at__gte='2024-01-01').filter(title__icontains='django')
```

Aggregation

Django also provides aggregation functions to perform calculations on your data. To use aggregation, you need to import the aggregate function from django.db.models:

```python
from django.db.models import Count, Avg
```

You can then use aggregation functions like Count and Avg:

```python
# Count the number of posts
post_count = Post.objects.count()

# Average length of the content in all posts
average_length = Post.objects.aggregate(Avg('content_length'))
```

Conclusion

In this chapter, you explored the fundamentals of Django models and databases. You learned how to define models, configure the database, create and apply migrations, and query the database using Django's powerful ORM. Understanding these concepts is essential for building robust and data-driven web applications with Django. In the next chapters, we will delve into the presentation layer with templates and explore how to create dynamic web pages.

Chapter 4: Building User Interfaces

In any web application, the user interface (UI) plays a crucial role in providing an interactive and visually appealing experience for users. Django makes it easy to build dynamic, data-driven UIs using templates, manage static and media files, and handle form submissions. In this chapter, we will explore how to build user interfaces in Django using templates, static files, media files, and forms.

4.1 Django Templates

Django uses a powerful templating engine to generate dynamic HTML. Templates are used to separate the presentation layer (HTML, CSS) from the logic and data handling (Python code), ensuring clean, maintainable code.

Key Features of Django Templates

- **Template Tags**: Django provides a set of built-in template tags that allow you to add logic to your templates. For example, you can loop over data, render dynamic content, and perform conditional checks.
- **Template Filters**: Filters allow you to modify values before they are displayed in the template. For example, you can format dates or truncate text.
- **Template Inheritance**: Django templates support inheritance, allowing

you to create a base template and extend it in child templates. This promotes reusability and consistency across your application.

4.1.1 Creating Template Files

To create and use a template in Django, follow these steps:

1. **Create a Templates Directory**: Inside your app's directory, create a templates folder. Inside this folder, you can create subfolders and organize your HTML files.

```arduino
myapp/
    templates/
        myapp/
            home.html
```

1. **Define a Template**: Create an HTML file (e.g., home.html) and add your HTML content:

```html
<!DOCTYPE html>
<html lang="en">
<head>
    <meta charset="UTF-8">
    <meta name="viewport" content="width=device-width, initial-scale=1.0">
    <title>Home Page</title>
</head>
<body>
```

```html
<h1>Welcome to the Home Page!</h1>
</body>
</html>
```

1. **Render the Template in a View**: In your views.py file, use Django's render() function to render the template:

python

```python
from django.shortcuts import render

def home(request):
    return render(request, 'myapp/home.html')
```

1. **Define a URL Pattern**: In your urls.py file, create a URL pattern to map the home view:

python

```python
from django.urls import path
from . import views

urlpatterns = [
    path('', views.home, name='home'),
]
```

When a user visits the root URL, Django will render the home.html template and display the content to the user.

4.1.2 Template Inheritance

One of the most powerful features of Django's templating engine is template inheritance. It allows you to define a base template with common elements (e.g., headers, footers) and extend it in other templates.

Creating a Base Template

1. **Define a Base Template**: Create a base.html file in the templates/myapp/ directory:

```html
<!DOCTYPE html>
<html lang="en">
<head>
    <meta charset="UTF-8">
    <meta name="viewport" content="width=device-width,
    initial-scale=1.0">
    <title>{% block title %}My Website{% endblock %}</title>
</head>
<body>
    <header>
        <h1>My Website Header</h1>
    </header>

    <main>
        {% block content %}{% endblock %}
    </main>

    <footer>
        <p>My Website Footer</p>
    </footer>
</body>
</html>
```

In this base template, we've defined two blocks: title and content. Child templates can override these blocks to provide their own content.

Extending the Base Template

1. **Extend the Base Template**: In home.html, extend the base.html template:

```html
{% extends 'myapp/base.html' %}

{% block title %}Home Page{% endblock %}

{% block content %}
<h1>Welcome to the Home Page!</h1>
<p>This is the homepage of my website.</p>
{% endblock %}
```

By using {% extends %}, the home.html template inherits the structure of base.html and provides its own content for the title and content blocks.

Benefits of Template Inheritance

- **Reusability**: Common elements like headers and footers can be defined once in the base template and reused across all child templates.
- **Consistency**: Ensures that all pages share a consistent structure and design.
- **Maintainability**: Changes to the layout (e.g., updating the footer) can be made in the base template, affecting all pages at once.

4.2 Static Files and Media Management

Static files such as CSS, JavaScript, and images are essential for designing and enhancing the appearance of your web application. Django provides mechanisms to manage both static files and user-uploaded media files.

4.2.1 Serving Static Files

Configuring Static Files

1. **Define STATIC_URL**: In your settings.py file, define the URL through which static files will be accessed:

```python
STATIC_URL = '/static/'
```

1. **Define STATICFILES_DIRS**: If you want to store static files in a custom directory (e.g., static/ in the project root), define it in settings.py:

```python
STATICFILES_DIRS = [
    BASE_DIR / 'static',
]
```

1. **Create a Static Directory**: In your project directory, create a static/ folder where you can store CSS, JavaScript, and image files.

```arduino
myproject/
    static/
        css/
            styles.css
```

Using Static Files in Templates

To include static files in your templates, use Django's {% static %} template tag. First, load the static template tag library at the top of your template:

```html
{% load static %}

<link rel="stylesheet"
  href="{% static 'css/styles.css' %}">
```

This ensures that Django knows where to find the static files.

Collecting Static Files (For Production)

In production, you need to collect all static files into a single directory using Django's collectstatic command:

```bash
python manage.py collectstatic
```

This will gather all static files from your app's static/ directories and place them in the directory specified by the STATIC_ROOT setting.

4.2.2 Handling User-Uploaded Files

Django provides built-in support for handling user-uploaded files, such as profile pictures or document uploads. These files are managed separately from static files.

Configuring Media Files

1. **Define MEDIA_URL and MEDIA_ROOT**: In your settings.py file, define the URL for serving media files and the directory where uploaded files will be stored:

```python
MEDIA_URL = '/media/'
MEDIA_ROOT = BASE_DIR / 'media'
```

1. **Create a Media Directory**: In your project directory, create a media/ folder where uploaded files will be stored.

Handling File Uploads in Models

To handle file uploads, use Django's FileField or ImageField in your model. Here's an example:

```python
from django.db import models

class Profile(models.Model):
    name = models.CharField(max_length=100)
    profile_picture = models.ImageField(upload_to='profile_pictures/')
```

The upload_to argument specifies the subdirectory within the media/ folder where the uploaded files will be saved.

Serving Media Files in Development

In development, you can serve media files by adding the following to your urls.py file:

```python
from django.conf import settings
from django.conf.urls.static import static
```

```
urlpatterns = [
    # other URL patterns
] + static(settings.MEDIA_URL,
document_root=settings.MEDIA_ROOT)
```

This allows Django to serve media files directly in development. In production, you will need to configure your web server (e.g., Nginx or Apache) to serve media files.

4.3 Form Handling

Forms are a key component of web applications, allowing users to submit data that can be processed and stored. Django provides an extensive framework for handling forms, including form validation and integration with models.

4.3.1 Creating Forms in Django

Django forms are defined as Python classes in the forms.py file. Here's an example of creating a simple contact form:

1. **Create a forms.py File**: In your app directory, create a forms.py file.
2. **Define a Form**:

python

```
from django import forms

class ContactForm(forms.Form):
    name = forms.CharField(max_length=100)
    email = forms.EmailField()
    message = forms.CharField(widget=forms.Textarea)
```

In this example, the ContactForm class defines three fields: name, email, and message. Each field is represented by a form field type (e.g., CharField, EmailField, Textarea).

4.3.2 Validating Form Data

Django automatically performs validation when a form is submitted. If the data does not meet the validation criteria, Django will return errors and redisplay the form with error messages.

Here's how you can handle form validation in a view:

python

```
from django.shortcuts import render
from .forms import ContactForm

def contact(request):
    if request.method == 'POST':
        form = ContactForm(request.POST)
        if form.is_valid():
            # Process the data
            name = form.cleaned_data['name']
            email = form.cleaned_data['email']
            message = form.cleaned_data['message']
            # Redirect or render success message
    else:
        form = ContactForm()

    return render(request, 'contact.html', {'form': form})
```

In this example, if the form is submitted via POST and passes validation, the data is available in form.cleaned_data.

4.3.3 Working with ModelForms

Django's ModelForm simplifies the creation of forms that are tied directly to models. It automatically generates form fields based on the model's fields.

Here's how to create a ModelForm:

1. **Import the Model and ModelForm**:

```python
from django import forms
from .models import Profile

class ProfileForm(forms.ModelForm):
    class Meta:
        model = Profile
        fields = ['name', 'profile_picture']
```

In this example, the ProfileForm class is tied to the Profile model and includes the name and profile_picture fields. When the form is submitted, Django will handle the validation and saving of the model instance.

Conclusion

In this chapter, you learned how to build user interfaces in Django using templates, manage static and media files, and handle form submissions. By mastering these concepts, you can create dynamic, interactive web applications with Django. In the next chapters, we'll explore more advanced topics such as user authentication, working with REST APIs, and optimizing your application for performance.

Chapter 5: User Authentication and Authorization

User authentication and authorization are essential components of any web application that involves user interaction, data privacy, or multi-tiered access control. Django simplifies this process by providing a robust, built-in authentication system that handles user login, registration, permissions, and password management. In this chapter, we will dive into Django's authentication framework and explore how to implement common features such as user registration, profile management, and password reset functionality.

5.1 Django's Built-in Authentication System

Django comes with a fully-featured authentication system that includes the following features:

- **User Authentication**: Verify a user's identity by checking credentials such as username and password.
- **User Authorization**: Control what actions a user can perform based on their permissions.
- **Sessions**: Manage logged-in users by storing session data.
- **Password Management**: Django includes functionality for setting,

changing, and resetting passwords.
- **Group and Permissions**: Fine-grained control over access to different parts of the application.

Django's authentication system revolves around the User model, which is provided by django.contrib.auth. It includes fields like username, email, password, first_name, and last_name.

Configuring Authentication

By default, Django includes django.contrib.auth in the INSTALLED_APPS setting, so you don't need to add it manually. To get started, ensure that the authentication system is enabled:

1. **Check INSTALLED_APPS**: In your settings.py file, ensure the following apps are listed:

```python
INSTALLED_APPS = [
    # Other apps
    'django.contrib.auth',
    'django.contrib.contenttypes',
    'django.contrib.sessions',
    'django.contrib.messages',
]
```

1. **Migrate the Database**: Django's authentication system creates database tables to store user information. Run the following command to apply the necessary migrations:

CHAPTER 5: USER AUTHENTICATION AND AUTHORIZATION

```bash
python manage.py migrate
```

User Authentication in Views

Django provides several built-in views for handling common authentication tasks, including login, logout, and password management.

Login

To implement user login functionality, use Django's built-in LoginView. First, add the login view to your urls.py file:

```python
from django.contrib.auth import views as auth_views
from django.urls import path

urlpatterns = [
    path('login/', auth_views.LoginView.as_view(), name='login'),
]
```

Next, create a login template in templates/registration/login.html:

```html
<form method="post">
    {% csrf_token %}
    {{ form.as_p }}
    <button type="submit">Login</button>
</form>
```

By default, Django expects the login template to be placed in the registration folder.

Logout

For user logout, use the built-in LogoutView. Add the logout view to your urls.py file:

```python
urlpatterns = [
    path('logout/', auth_views.
LogoutView.as_view(), name='logout'),
]
```

To handle redirection after logout, add the following to your settings.py file:

```python
LOGOUT_REDIRECT_URL = '/'
```

This redirects users to the homepage after logging out.

5.2 User Registration and Profile Management

User registration involves creating a new user account and optionally setting up a user profile. Django makes this process straightforward by allowing you to extend the User model with custom fields and forms.

User Registration

To allow users to sign up for an account, you need to create a registration form, a view to handle the form submission, and a URL pattern to connect it.
 Create a Registration Form
 In your app's forms.py file, create a registration form using Django's UserCreationForm:

CHAPTER 5: USER AUTHENTICATION AND AUTHORIZATION

python

```
from django import forms
from django.contrib.auth.forms import UserCreationForm
from django.contrib.auth.models import User

class RegisterForm(UserCreationForm):
    email = forms.EmailField(required=True)

    class Meta:
        model = User
        fields = ['username', 'email', 'password1', 'password2']
```

This form extends UserCreationForm and adds an email field. The password1 and password2 fields handle password confirmation.

Create a Registration View

In your views.py file, create a view to handle the registration form:

python

```
from django.shortcuts import render, redirect
from django.contrib.auth import login
from .forms import RegisterForm

def register(request):
    if request.method == 'POST':
        form = RegisterForm(request.POST)
        if form.is_valid():
            user = form.save()
            login(request, user)
            return redirect('home')
    else:
        form = RegisterForm()
    return render(request, 'registration/register.html', {'form': form})
```

This view checks whether the form submission is valid and logs in the user automatically after successful registration.

Create a Registration Template

Create a registration template at templates/registration/register.html:

html

```
<form method="post">
    {% csrf_token %}
    {{ form.as_p }}
    <button type="submit">Register</button>
</form>
```

Add a URL Pattern for Registration

Finally, add the URL pattern for the registration view in your urls.py file:

python

```
urlpatterns = [
    path('register/', views.register, name='register'),
]
```

Profile Management

After registration, users may want to manage their profiles. You can extend the User model to include additional profile information by creating a Profile model and linking it to the User model with a one-to-one relationship.

Create a Profile Model

In models.py, define the Profile model:

python

```
from django.db import models
from django.contrib.auth.models import User
```

```python
class Profile(models.Model):
    user = models.OneToOneField(User, on_delete=models.CASCADE)
    bio = models.TextField(max_length=500, blank=True)
    location = models.CharField(max_length=100, blank=True)

    def __str__(self):
        return self.user.username
```

This model stores additional user information, such as a bio and location.

Signals for Profile Creation

To automatically create a Profile when a new User is registered, use Django signals:

python

```
from django.db.models.signals import post_save
from django.dispatch import receiver
from .models import Profile

@receiver(post_save, sender=User)
def create_profile(sender, instance, created, **kwargs):
    if created:
        Profile.objects.create(user=instance)

@receiver(post_save, sender=User)
def save_profile(sender, instance, **kwargs):
    instance.profile.save()
```

5.3 Managing User Permissions

In Django, permissions determine what actions a user can perform in the application. By default, Django provides three permissions for each model: add, change, and delete. You can also create custom permissions and assign them to users or groups.

Assigning Permissions

Permissions can be assigned either to individual users or to groups of users. Here's an example of how to assign permissions to a user:

python

```
from django.contrib.auth.models import User, Permission

user = User.objects.get(username='johndoe')
permission = Permission.objects.get(codename='can_add_post')
user.user_permissions.add(permission)
```

Checking Permissions in Views

To check if a user has a specific permission in a view, use the has_perm() method:

python

```
if request.user.has_perm('myapp.can_add_post'):
    # User has the permission
```

Alternatively, you can use the permission_required decorator to restrict access to views:

python

```
from django.contrib.auth.decorators import permission_required

@permission_required('myapp.can_add_post')
def add_post(request):
    # View logic
```

Group Permissions

Groups allow you to assign a set of permissions to multiple users at once. For example, you can create an Editors group and assign it specific permissions:

```python
from django.contrib.auth.models import Group, Permission

editors_group = Group.objects.create(name='Editors')
permission = Permission.objects.get(codename='can_edit_post')
editors_group.permissions.add(permission)
```

Users can be added to the group, and they will inherit the group's permissions:

```python
user.groups.add(editors_group)
```

5.4 Implementing Password Reset and Change

Django provides built-in views and templates for handling password reset and password change functionality.

Password Change

The password change functionality allows logged-in users to change their passwords. Django's PasswordChangeView and PasswordChangeDoneView handle this process.

1. **Add URL Patterns**: In your urls.py file, add the following URL patterns:

```python
from django.contrib.auth import views as auth_views

urlpatterns = [
    path('password_change/', auth_views.PasswordChangeView.as_view(), name='password_change'),
    path('password_change/done/',
        auth_views.PasswordChangeDoneView.as_view(),
        name='password_change_done'),
]
```

1. **Create Templates**: Create the corresponding templates at templates/registration/password_change_form.html and templates/registration/password_change_done.html.

Password Reset

Password reset allows users who have forgotten their passwords to request a reset email and set a new password. Django's built-in views handle the entire process, including sending the reset email.

1. **Add URL Patterns**: In your urls.py file, add the following URL patterns:

```python
urlpatterns = [
    path('password_reset/', auth_views.PasswordResetView.as_view(), name='password_reset'),
    path('password_reset/done/',
        auth_views.PasswordResetDoneView.as_view(),
        name='password_reset_done'),
    path('reset/<uidb64>/<token>/',
        auth_views.PasswordResetConfirmView.as_view(),
```

```
            name='password_reset_confirm'),
      path('reset/done/',
            auth_views.PasswordResetCompleteView.as_view(),
            name='password_reset_complete'),
]
```

1. **Create Templates**: Create the required templates in the registration folder:

   - password_reset_form.html
   - password_reset_done.html
   - password_reset_confirm.html
   - password_reset_complete.html

Django will handle sending the reset email to the user, and the user can follow the link in the email to reset their password.

Configuring Email Settings

To enable password reset functionality, you need to configure your email settings in settings.py:

```python
EMAIL_BACKEND = 'django.core.mail.backends.smtp.EmailBackend'
EMAIL_HOST = 'smtp.example.com'
EMAIL_PORT = 587
EMAIL_USE_TLS = True
EMAIL_HOST_USER = 'your-email@example.com'
EMAIL_HOST_PASSWORD = 'your-password'
```

You can also use Django's console email backend during development:

```python
EMAIL_BACKEND = 'django.core.mail.
backends.console.EmailBackend'
```

Conclusion

In this chapter, we explored Django's built-in authentication system, including how to implement user login, registration, profile management, and password reset functionality. We also discussed managing user permissions and groups. These are essential features for any web application that requires user accounts and role-based access control. In the next chapter, we will dive into more advanced topics like REST APIs and handling asynchronous tasks.

Chapter 6: Advanced Django Features

Django provides a wealth of advanced features that allow developers to build more robust, efficient, and maintainable applications. These features include the ability to customize the Django admin interface, work with middleware, improve performance with caching, and handle application events using Django signals. In this chapter, we will explore these advanced Django features and how they can be used to enhance your application.

6.1 Django Admin Customization

The Django admin interface is one of the most powerful features of Django. It provides a full-fledged management system for your application's data and can be customized to meet specific project requirements. Out of the box, the admin interface is generic but can be tailored to improve usability and functionality.

Registering Models in the Admin

To make your models accessible via the Django admin interface, you need to register them in your app's admin.py file.

Here's how to register a simple model:

python

```
from django.contrib import admin
from .models import Post

admin.site.register(Post)
```

Once registered, the Post model will appear in the admin interface, allowing you to add, edit, and delete posts through the UI.

Customizing Model Admin

Django allows you to customize how your models are displayed and managed in the admin interface using the ModelAdmin class. You can specify fields, search capabilities, filters, and more.

Customizing the List Display

You can customize which fields are shown in the list view of your model in the admin interface. In admin.py, modify the ModelAdmin class:

python

```
@admin.register(Post)
class PostAdmin(admin.ModelAdmin):
    list_display = ('title', 'author', 'created_at', 'status')
    list_filter = ('status', 'created_at')
    search_fields = ('title', 'content')
    ordering = ['created_at']
```

- **list_display**: Defines the fields that will be shown in the list view.
- **list_filter**: Adds filters to the sidebar based on specific fields.
- **search_fields**: Enables a search bar to search through specific fields.
- **ordering**: Sets the default ordering of the list.

Inline Editing of Related Models

If you have related models (e.g., a Comment model related to a Post model), you can enable inline editing of the related model within the parent model's admin page:

```python
from .models import Comment

class CommentInline(admin.TabularInline):
    model = Comment
    extra = 1

@admin.register(Post)
class PostAdmin(admin.ModelAdmin):
    inlines = [CommentInline]
```

This allows you to manage related models directly on the same page as the parent model.

Customizing the Admin Template

You can also override the default admin templates if you need to customize the look and feel of the admin interface. Admin templates are located in django/contrib/admin/templates/admin/. You can override these templates by creating a corresponding file in your project's template directory:

```bash
myproject/
    templates/
        admin/
            base_site.html
```

For example, you could customize the base admin template (base_site.html) to add your own branding or design elements.

Conclusion of Admin Customization

Django's admin interface is a powerful tool that can be customized extensively to suit your needs. By tweaking the list display, adding filters, inline editing, and even customizing the admin templates, you can turn the default admin interface into a highly functional backend for your application.

6.2 Middleware and Request Processing

Middleware in Django is a way to process requests and responses globally. Middleware components are hooks that can alter the request or response objects at different stages of processing. They are applied to every request that comes into your Django application.

How Middleware Works

When a request comes into your Django application, it passes through a series of middleware components before reaching the view. Each middleware can modify the request or the response. Middleware can be thought of as a stack that the request travels through on the way in and the response travels back through on the way out.

Creating Custom Middleware

You can create your own custom middleware to handle specific request processing tasks. Middleware is defined as a Python class with __call__() method to handle the request and response:

```python
class CustomMiddleware:
    def __init__(self, get_response):
        self.get_response = get_response
```

```python
def __call__(self, request):
    # Pre-process the request
    print("Custom middleware executed before the view")

    # Call the next middleware or view
    response = self.get_response(request)

    # Post-process the response
    print("Custom middleware executed after the view")

    return response
```

This middleware will execute before and after every request that hits your application. To use it, you need to add it to the MIDDLEWARE setting in settings.py:

```python
MIDDLEWARE = [
    # Other middleware
    'myapp.middleware.CustomMiddleware',
]
```

Common Use Cases for Middleware

- **Authentication**: Middleware can be used to enforce authentication across your application by redirecting unauthenticated users.
- **Logging and Analytics**: Track and log request/response details for performance analysis or auditing.
- **CORS (Cross-Origin Resource Sharing)**: Middleware can handle cross-origin resource sharing (CORS) by adding headers to responses.
- **Session Management**: Middleware can be used to manage session handling or extend the session functionality in Django.

6.3 Caching Strategies for Performance

Caching is an essential strategy for improving the performance of your Django application. Caching reduces the time it takes to serve a page by storing and reusing expensive or frequently accessed data.

Types of Caching in Django

Django provides several levels of caching that you can implement:

1. **View-Level Caching**: Cache the entire output of a view.
2. **Template Fragment Caching**: Cache specific parts of a template.
3. **Low-Level Caching**: Manually store and retrieve arbitrary data in the cache.

Configuring Django Caching

To configure caching, you need to set up the cache backend in your settings.py. Django supports various cache backends, including Memcached, Redis, and local file-based caching.

Here's an example of configuring a memory-based cache using Memcached:

```python
CACHES = {
    'default': {
        'BACKEND':
        'django.core.cache.backends.memcached.MemcachedCache',
        'LOCATION': '127.0.0.1:11211',
    }
}
```

CHAPTER 6: ADVANCED DJANGO FEATURES

View-Level Caching

View-level caching is the simplest way to implement caching in Django. It caches the entire response of a view for a specified amount of time.

Here's an example of applying view-level caching to a view:

```python
from django.views.decorators.cache import cache_page

@cache_page(60 * 15)  # Cache for 15 minutes
def my_view(request):
    # View logic
    return render(request, 'myapp/template.html')
```

Template Fragment Caching

Sometimes you don't want to cache the entire page, but only specific parts of it. Django allows you to cache specific template fragments:

```html
{% load cache %}
{% cache 600 sidebar %}
    <!-- Expensive sidebar content -->
{% endcache %}
```

This will cache the sidebar for 600 seconds (10 minutes), while the rest of the page remains dynamic.

Low-Level Caching

For more control over what is cached and when, you can use Django's low-level caching API. This allows you to cache arbitrary data, such as query results or expensive calculations:

```python
from django.core.cache import cache

# Store data in the cache
cache.set('my_key', 'my_value', timeout=60)

# Retrieve data from the cache
value = cache.get('my_key')
```

Cache Invalidation

One of the challenges of caching is ensuring that cached data is invalidated (i.e., removed or updated) when it becomes stale. Django's caching system allows you to set timeouts for cache entries or manually clear the cache when needed:

```python
cache.delete('my_key')   # Delete a specific cache entry
cache.clear()            # Clear the entire cache
```

6.4 Working with Django Signals

Django signals provide a way for decoupled applications to get notified when certain events happen in the application. They allow different parts of your app to communicate without requiring direct dependencies.

What Are Signals?

Signals are especially useful for triggering specific actions when something happens, such as a user logging in or saving an object to the database. Django provides several built-in signals, but you can also define your own custom signals.

Built-in Signals

Django provides several built-in signals, including:

- **pre_save**: Sent before a model's save() method is called.
- **post_save**: Sent after a model's save() method is called.
- **pre_delete**: Sent before a model's delete() method is called.
- **post_delete**: Sent after a model's delete() method is called.
- **request_started**: Sent when Django starts processing an HTTP request.
- **request_finished**: Sent when Django finishes processing an HTTP request.

Connecting to a Signal

To connect a signal to a function, you use the @receiver decorator. For example, to execute code after a user is saved:

```python
from django.db.models.signals import post_save
from django.dispatch import receiver
from django.contrib.auth.models import User

@receiver(post_save, sender=User)
def user_saved(sender, instance, created, **kwargs):
    if created:
        print(f"User {
```

Chapter 7: RESTful APIs with Django

RESTful APIs are the backbone of modern web applications, allowing different systems to communicate with each other by exchanging data. Django, combined with the Django REST Framework (DRF), makes it easy to build robust APIs that follow REST principles. In this chapter, we will cover the essentials of RESTful APIs, setting up Django REST Framework, building API endpoints, and testing them.

7.1 Introduction to REST and APIs

What is REST?

REST (Representational State Transfer) is an architectural style for designing networked applications. RESTful services provide a way to expose data and functionality to external systems over HTTP, typically in a stateless manner. REST is built around a few key principles:

- **Stateless**: Each request from a client to the server must contain all the information needed to process the request, with no reliance on previous requests.
- **Resource-based**: In REST, everything is treated as a resource. Resources are identified by URIs (Uniform Resource Identifiers).
- **HTTP Methods**: RESTful APIs use HTTP methods (GET, POST, PUT,

DELETE) to perform operations on resources:
- **GET**: Retrieve data from a resource.
- **POST**: Create a new resource.
- **PUT**: Update an existing resource.
- **DELETE**: Remove a resource.

REST vs Traditional Web Applications

Traditional web applications typically return HTML rendered on the server, while REST APIs return data (often in JSON or XML format) that can be consumed by a variety of clients, including web browsers, mobile apps, and third-party services. This separation of frontend and backend allows for more flexibility and scalability in building applications.

Use Cases for REST APIs

- **Mobile Applications**: APIs allow mobile apps to communicate with a server, retrieve or update data, and perform other operations.
- **Third-Party Integrations**: External services can interact with your application by consuming your API.
- **Single-Page Applications (SPAs)**: SPAs often use REST APIs to fetch data dynamically without reloading the page.

7.2 Setting Up Django REST Framework

The **Django REST Framework (DRF)** is a powerful toolkit that allows you to build APIs quickly and efficiently. It provides features such as serialization, authentication, and customizable viewsets for creating RESTful APIs in Django.

Installing Django REST Framework

To start building RESTful APIs, you need to install Django REST Framework. In your terminal, run the following command:

```bash
pip install djangorestframework
```

After installing, add rest_framework to the INSTALLED_APPS in your settings.py:

```python
INSTALLED_APPS = [
    # Other installed apps
    'rest_framework',
]
```

Basic Configuration

You can configure Django REST Framework settings in settings.py. Here's an example configuration:

```python
REST_FRAMEWORK = {
    'DEFAULT_AUTHENTICATION_CLASSES': [
        'rest_framework.authentication.SessionAuthentication',
        'rest_framework.authentication.TokenAuthentication',
    ],
    'DEFAULT_PERMISSION_CLASSES': [
        'rest_framework.permissions.IsAuthenticated',
    ]
```

}

This configuration ensures that only authenticated users can access the API. You can customize the authentication and permission settings based on your project's needs.

7.3 Building API Endpoints

API endpoints are the URLs where your application exposes resources. Django REST Framework provides tools like **serializers**, **views**, and **routers** to help you build and manage these endpoints efficiently.

7.3.1 Serializers

Serializers in Django REST Framework are similar to Django forms. They allow you to convert complex data types, such as querysets or model instances, into JSON or other content types that can be returned via an API. They also handle data validation for input coming into the API.

Defining a Serializer

To create a serializer, define a class in your app's serializers.py file:

```python
from rest_framework import serializers
from .models import Post

class PostSerializer(serializers.ModelSerializer):
    class Meta:
        model = Post
        fields = ['id', 'title',
'content', 'author', 'created_at']
```

In this example, the PostSerializer converts the Post model into JSON format. The ModelSerializer automatically generates fields based on the model's definition.

7.3.2 ViewSets and Routers

Django REST Framework provides **ViewSets** to handle the logic for different HTTP methods (GET, POST, PUT, DELETE) in a single class. ViewSets are a powerful abstraction that simplifies the code needed for building REST APIs.

Creating a ViewSet

Here's how to create a simple viewset for the Post model:

python

```python
from rest_framework import viewsets
from .models import Post
from .serializers import PostSerializer

class PostViewSet(viewsets.ModelViewSet):
    queryset = Post.objects.all()
    serializer_class = PostSerializer
```

In this example, PostViewSet inherits from ModelViewSet, which provides default implementations for common CRUD operations (create, read, update, delete).

Registering Routes with Routers

Django REST Framework provides **routers** to automatically generate URL patterns for your viewsets. In your app's urls.py file, you can register the viewsets with a router:

python

```python
from rest_framework.routers import DefaultRouter
from .views import PostViewSet

router = DefaultRouter()
router.register(r'posts', PostViewSet)

urlpatterns = [
    # Other URL patterns
```

```
    path('', include(router.urls)),
]
```

The router automatically generates RESTful endpoints for your viewset:

- GET /posts/ – Retrieve all posts.
- GET /posts/{id}/ – Retrieve a single post.
- POST /posts/ – Create a new post.
- PUT /posts/{id}/ – Update a post.
- DELETE /posts/{id}/ – Delete a post.

Customizing ViewSets

You can customize the behavior of your viewset by overriding its methods or adding custom actions. For example, to restrict a viewset to only GET requests, you can modify the PostViewSet:

python

```
class PostViewSet(viewsets.ModelViewSet):
    queryset = Post.objects.all()
    serializer_class = PostSerializer
    http_method_names = ['get', 'head']
```

Custom actions can also be added using the @action decorator:

python

```
from rest_framework.decorators import action
from rest_framework.response import Response

class PostViewSet(viewsets.ModelViewSet):
    queryset = Post.objects.all()
    serializer_class = PostSerializer
```

```
    @action(detail=False, methods=['get'])
    def recent(self, request):
        recent_posts = Post.objects.
filter(created_at__gte='2024-01-01')
        serializer = self.get_serializer
(recent_posts, many=True)
        return Response(serializer.data)
```

This custom action, recent, retrieves posts created after a specific date. You can access it via GET /posts/recent/.

7.4 Testing Your API

Testing is an essential part of developing APIs to ensure that endpoints are working correctly and returning the expected data. Django REST Framework provides tools for testing your APIs.

Using Django's Test Framework

You can use Django's built-in testing framework to write unit tests for your API. Here's an example of how to test a GET request to the Post API:

```python
from django.urls import reverse
from rest_framework import status
from rest_framework.test import APITestCase
from .models import Post

class PostTests(APITestCase):
    def test_get_posts(self):
        url = reverse('post-list')  # Generated by the router
        response = self.client.get(url)
        self.assertEqual(response.
status_code, status.HTTP_200_OK)
```

In this test, we use the APITestCase class provided by Django REST Framework to simulate a GET request to the Post API. The reverse() function is used to get the URL for the viewset, and we verify that the response returns an HTTP 200 status code.

Testing with cURL

You can also use command-line tools like **cURL** to test your API endpoints. For example, to retrieve a list of posts, you can run the following cURL command:

```bash
curl -X GET http://127.0.0.1:8000/posts/
```

To create a new post, you can use the following command:

```bash
curl -X POST http://127.0.0.1:8000/posts/ -d "title=New Post&content=This is a new post"
```

This is a quick way to interact with your API and test the different endpoints manually.

Using Postman for API Testing

Postman is a popular tool for testing APIs with a graphical interface. It allows you to send requests to your API, view responses, and manage collections of API requests. You can easily test the behavior of your endpoints by entering the URL, selecting the HTTP method (GET, POST, PUT, DELETE), and viewing the response.

Here's how to use Postman to test your API:

1. Download and install Postman.

2. Create a new request.
3. Enter the API endpoint URL (e.g., http://127.0.0.1:8000/posts/).
4. Select the HTTP method (e.g., GET).
5. Click **Send** to see the API response.

Conclusion

In this chapter, you learned how to set up Django REST Framework, build API endpoints using serializers, viewsets, and routers, and test your APIs. These concepts are critical for building robust and scalable RESTful services in Django.

Chapter 8: Deployment and Maintenance

Deploying a Django application to a production environment involves several steps to ensure the application is secure, performant, and scalable. This chapter will guide you through the process of preparing your Django project for production, managing security best practices, and handling static and media files.

8.1 Preparing for Production

Before deploying a Django application to production, several configurations must be applied to ensure that your application runs smoothly and securely. The default development settings are not suitable for production, so it is crucial to modify these settings and prepare your project appropriately.

8.1.1 Security Best Practices

Security is one of the most critical aspects of deploying a web application. Django provides several security features that you should enable or configure in a production environment.

1. Disable Debug Mode

Debug mode in Django provides detailed error messages and stack traces, which are useful during development but should never be enabled in production because they expose sensitive information.

In your settings.py file, set DEBUG to False:

python

```
DEBUG = False
```

When DEBUG is set to False, Django will show custom error pages rather than detailed technical information.

2. Set Allowed Hosts

The ALLOWED_HOSTS setting defines a whitelist of domain names or IP addresses that can serve your Django app. If a request comes from an unlisted host, Django will return an HTTP 400 (Bad Request) response.

In settings.py, define the allowed hosts:

python

```
ALLOWED_HOSTS = ['yourdomain.com',
'www.yourdomain.com', '127.0.0.1']
```

Ensure that only the domains you are serving the application from are listed here.

3. Use Secure Cookies

To prevent certain types of attacks, you should secure cookies by setting the following options in your settings.py:

- **SESSION_COOKIE_SECURE**: Ensures cookies are only sent over HTTPS.
- **CSRF_COOKIE_SECURE**: Ensures the CSRF cookie is only sent over HTTPS.

python

```
SESSION_COOKIE_SECURE = True
CSRF_COOKIE_SECURE = True
```

Both settings ensure that cookies are sent over secure connections only, reducing the risk of attacks like man-in-the-middle.

4. Enable HTTPS

Your Django app should always run over HTTPS in production to protect data during transmission. To enforce HTTPS, consider setting the following headers:

```python
SECURE_SSL_REDIRECT = True
 # Redirect all HTTP requests to HTTPS
SECURE_HSTS_SECONDS = 31536000
 # Use HTTP Strict Transport Security
SECURE_HSTS_INCLUDE_SUBDOMAINS =
True  # Apply HSTS to subdomains
SECURE_HSTS_PRELOAD = True
 # Preload HSTS policy in supported browsers
```

The SECURE_HSTS_SECONDS option defines how long browsers should remember to access your site only via HTTPS. The SECURE_HSTS_PRELOAD option allows your domain to be preloaded into browsers' HSTS lists.

5. CSRF and XSS Protection

Cross-Site Request Forgery (CSRF) and Cross-Site Scripting (XSS) are common attacks that target web applications. Django provides protection against these attacks by default, but you need to ensure they are enabled:

- **CSRF**: Django automatically includes CSRF protection for all forms that use the {% csrf_token %} template tag. You should ensure this tag is present in all forms.
- **XSS**: Use Django's built-in escaping functions to prevent XSS attacks. Django automatically escapes variables in templates unless explicitly marked as safe.

6. Secure Database Connections

If your application connects to a remote database, ensure that the connection is encrypted. You can achieve this by enabling SSL for your database connection.

For example, to secure a PostgreSQL connection, add the following options to your database settings:

```python
DATABASES = {
    'default': {
        'ENGINE': 'django.db.backends.postgresql',
        'NAME': 'your_db_name',
        'USER': 'your_db_user',
        'PASSWORD': 'your_password',
        'HOST': 'your_db_host',
        'PORT': '5432',
        'OPTIONS': {
            'sslmode': 'require',
        },
    }
}
```

7. Use Environment Variables for Sensitive Data

Do not store sensitive information like passwords, API keys, or secret keys directly in your settings.py file. Instead, use environment variables to manage sensitive data.

You can use the python-decouple package to handle environment variables:

```bash
pip install python-decouple
```

Then, update your settings.py:

```python
from decouple import config

SECRET_KEY = config('SECRET_KEY')
DEBUG = config('DEBUG', default=False, cast=bool)
DATABASES = {
    'default': {
        'ENGINE': 'django.db.backends.postgresql',
        'NAME': config('DB_NAME'),
        'USER': config('DB_USER'),
        'PASSWORD': config('DB_PASSWORD'),
        'HOST': config('DB_HOST'),
        'PORT': config('DB_PORT', default='5432'),
    }
}
```

Create a .env file to store environment variables:

```bash
SECRET_KEY=your_secret_key
DEBUG=False
DB_NAME=your_db_name
DB_USER=your_db_user
DB_PASSWORD=your_db_password
DB_HOST=your_db_host
DB_PORT=5432
```

This approach keeps your sensitive data secure and separate from your codebase.

8.1.2 Static and Media File Management

Handling static files (CSS, JavaScript, images) and media files (user-uploaded content) in production is different from how you manage them in development. In development, Django serves static and media files directly, but in production, you need a more efficient solution.

1. Collecting Static Files

In a production environment, static files need to be collected in a single directory so they can be served efficiently. This is done using Django's collectstatic command.

In your settings.py, configure the directory where static files will be collected:

python

```
STATIC_URL = '/static/'
STATIC_ROOT = BASE_DIR / 'staticfiles'
```

Run the collectstatic command to collect all static files into the STATIC_ROOT directory:

bash

```
python manage.py collectstatic
```

After running this command, you need to configure your web server (e.g., Nginx or Apache) to serve static files from the staticfiles/ directory.

2. Serving Static Files with Nginx

Nginx is commonly used to serve static files in a production environment. You can configure Nginx to serve static files by adding the following block to your Nginx configuration file:

nginx

```
server {
    location /static/ {
        alias /path/to/your/staticfiles/;
    }
}
```

This configuration tells Nginx to serve static files from the staticfiles/

CHAPTER 8: DEPLOYMENT AND MAINTENANCE

directory when a request is made to /static/.

3. Managing Media Files

Media files, which are typically user-uploaded content, are handled separately from static files. In your settings.py, configure the directory where media files will be stored:

```python
MEDIA_URL = '/media/'
MEDIA_ROOT = BASE_DIR / 'media'
```

For production, you also need to configure your web server to serve media files. If you're using Nginx, add the following block to your configuration:

```nginx
server {
    location /media/ {
        alias /path/to/your/media/
```

Chapter 9: Testing in Django

Testing is a critical part of the development process, ensuring that your application works as expected and that new changes don't introduce bugs. Django comes with a built-in testing framework that allows you to write and run tests for your project. This chapter will cover the importance of testing, unit testing in Django, how to test views and forms, and the use of factories for generating test data.

9.1 Importance of Testing

Testing helps ensure the correctness, stability, and maintainability of your Django application. Without proper testing, changes to code can introduce unexpected bugs and regressions, leading to increased development time and potential issues in production.

Key Benefits of Testing

- **Reliability**: Testing ensures that your code behaves as expected under different conditions, reducing the chance of errors in production.
- **Regression Prevention**: Automated tests help catch bugs early when new features are added or existing code is modified.
- **Maintainability**: Tests act as documentation for your code, making it easier for other developers (or future you) to understand and modify the

application.
- **Confidence in Refactoring**: When refactoring or optimizing code, having tests in place ensures that the refactored code doesn't break existing functionality.
- **Automation**: Automated tests allow you to verify the correctness of your application with minimal effort, as opposed to manually checking each feature.

Django's testing framework encourages the use of unit tests to check the smallest units of your application, as well as functional tests to verify that your views, forms, and models behave as expected.

9.2 Unit Testing and Test Cases

Django's testing framework is built on top of Python's unittest module. A unit test verifies the behavior of individual units of code, such as functions or methods. Each test case represents a specific scenario that the unit of code should handle correctly.

Creating a Test Case

In Django, test cases are written in a tests.py file inside your app. Here's an example of a simple unit test:

1. **Define a Test Case**: Create a test case class that inherits from django.test.TestCase or unittest.TestCase.

```python
from django.test import TestCase
from .models import Post
```

```
class PostModelTest(TestCase):
    def test_create_post(self):
        post = Post.objects.
create(title="Test Post", content="This is a test.")
        self.assertEqual(post.title, "Test Post")
```

In this example, the test verifies that a Post instance can be created successfully and that its title field is set correctly.

Running Unit Tests

To run all tests in your Django project, use the following command:

bash

```
python manage.py test
```

This will automatically discover all test cases in your project and execute them. Django will set up a temporary test database to ensure that the tests don't affect your actual data.

Common Assertions in Unit Testing

Django provides several assertion methods to check whether certain conditions are true. Here are some commonly used assertions:

- **self.assertEqual(a, b)**: Asserts that a is equal to b.
- **self.assertTrue(x)**: Asserts that x is True.
- **self.assertFalse(x)**: Asserts that x is False.
- **self.assertIn(a, b)**: Asserts that a is in b.
- **self.assertRaises(exception)**: Asserts that a specific exception is raised.

For example, to check that an exception is raised when an invalid operation occurs:

```python
def test_invalid_operation(self):
    with self.assertRaises(ValueError):
        invalid_value = int("invalid")
```

9.3 Testing Views and Forms

Testing views and forms ensures that your application's user-facing functionality works as expected, including how data is processed and rendered in templates. Django provides tools to simulate HTTP requests and validate form submissions during testing.

Testing Views

Testing views involves simulating HTTP requests to your application and verifying the responses. Django's TestCase class provides a client that can be used to simulate GET and POST requests to your views.

Testing a Simple View

Here's how to test a view that renders a list of blog posts:

```python
from django.urls import reverse
from django.test import TestCase
from .models import Post

class PostListViewTest(TestCase):
    def setUp(self):
        Post.objects.create(title="First Post", content="First post content")
        Post.objects.create
```

```
(title="Second Post", content="Second post content")

    def test_post_list_view(self):
        response = self.client.get(reverse('post-list'))
        self.assertEqual(response.status_code, 200)
        self.assertContains(response, "First Post")
        self.assertContains(response, "Second Post")
```

In this example:

- **self.client.get()**: Simulates a GET request to the post-list view.
- **self.assertEqual()**: Verifies that the response has an HTTP 200 status code (OK).
- **self.assertContains()**: Checks if the response contains specific content.

Testing a POST Request

To test a view that handles form submissions, simulate a POST request:

python

```
def test_create_post_view(self):
    response = self.client.post(reverse('post-create'), {
        'title': 'New Post',
        'content': 'New post content',
    })
    self.assertEqual(response.status_code, 302)
# Should redirect after a successful form submission
    self.assertTrue(Post.objects.
filter(title='New Post').exists())
```

This test submits a POST request to the post-create view and checks that a new post is created in the database.

Testing Forms

Testing forms involves checking form validation and how the form processes input data. You can directly test form validation by creating form instances and passing different sets of data.

Testing Form Validation

Here's an example of testing a form:

```python
from django.test import TestCase
from .forms import PostForm

class PostFormTest(TestCase):
    def test_valid_form(self):
        form_data = {'title': 'Test Post',
'content': 'This is a test post.'}
        form = PostForm(data=form_data)
        self.assertTrue(form.is_valid())

    def test_invalid_form(self):
        form_data = {'title': '',
'content': 'This is a test post.'}
        form = PostForm(data=form_data)
        self.assertFalse(form.is_valid())
```

- **form.is_valid()**: Checks if the form data is valid based on the validation rules defined in the form class.
- **self.assertTrue()**: Asserts that the form is valid in the first test case.
- **self.assertFalse()**: Asserts that the form is invalid due to a missing title in the second test case.

9.4 Using Factories for Test Data

When testing models, it's often necessary to generate test data. Writing repetitive code to create model instances can be time-consuming and error-prone. Factories help simplify the process of generating test data.

What is a Factory?

A factory is a design pattern used to create objects without having to specify the exact class of the object that will be created. In testing, factories allow you to generate model instances with predefined values.

The **Factory Boy** library is commonly used with Django for generating test data. To install it, run:

```bash
pip install factory_boy
```

Creating a Factory

Here's how to create a factory for the Post model:

```python
import factory
from .models import Post

class PostFactory(factory.django.DjangoModelFactory):
    class Meta:
        model = Post

    title = factory.Faker('sentence')
```

```
content = factory.Faker('paragraph')
```

In this example, the factory uses Faker to generate random titles and content for the Post model.

Using Factories in Tests

Once you have defined a factory, you can use it to generate test data in your tests:

python

```
from django.test import TestCase
from .models import Post
from .factories import PostFactory

class PostFactoryTest(TestCase):
    def test_post_factory(self):
        post = PostFactory()
        self.assertIsInstance(post, Post)
        self.assertTrue(Post.objects.filter(title=post.title).exists())
```

The factory allows you to quickly create test data, making your test cases cleaner and more maintainable. You can also customize factory instances by passing specific data:

python

```
custom_post = PostFactory(title="Custom Title")
self.assertEqual(custom_post.title, "Custom Title")
```

Benefits of Using Factories

- **Reduces Boilerplate Code**: Factories allow you to avoid manually creating instances of models, especially when creating test data for multiple models.
- **Reusable**: Factories can be reused across multiple test cases, ensuring consistency in test data.
- **Customizable**: You can customize the generated data while still leveraging the factory's default behavior.

Conclusion

In this chapter, we explored the importance of testing in Django applications, focusing on unit testing, testing views and forms, and using factories to generate test data. By incorporating these practices into your workflow, you can ensure the stability, reliability, and maintainability of your Django application. In the next chapters, we will explore more advanced topics like performance optimization and working with asynchronous tasks.

Chapter 10: Best Practices and Patterns

Maintaining high code quality and following best practices is essential for building scalable, maintainable, and efficient Django applications. In this chapter, we will explore best practices for project structure, code quality and style, performance optimization, and managing environment variables effectively.

10.1 Project Structure Best Practices

A well-organized project structure improves code readability, maintainability, and collaboration, especially as the project grows. Django projects are typically organized by apps, and each app is designed to handle a specific aspect of the application.

Django's Default Project Structure

Here is the default structure generated by startproject:

```markdown
myproject/
    manage.py
    myproject/
```

```
__init__.py
settings.py
urls.py
wsgi.py
asgi.py
```

Each app inside the project will have its own directory, usually generated with startapp:

```arduino
myapp/
    migrations/
    templates/
    static/
    __init__.py
    admin.py
    apps.py
    models.py
    views.py
    urls.py
```

While this structure is effective for small projects, as your project scales, you may need additional organization.

Structuring Large Projects

For larger projects, consider organizing apps by domain or functionality. A common approach is to group related functionality together:

```csharp
myproject/
    apps/
        blog/
```

```
        models.py
        views.py
        admin.py
        urls.py
    users/
        models.py
        views.py
        admin.py
        urls.py
static/
templates/
manage.py
myproject/
    settings/
        base.py
        production.py
        development.py
```

Key Best Practices

1. **Separate Settings for Different Environments**: As your project grows, it's important to have separate settings for different environments (development, testing, production). Instead of a single settings.py file, break it down:

- base.py for shared settings
- development.py for development-specific settings
- production.py for production settings

1. **Modular Apps**: Ensure that each app is responsible for one specific feature. This makes it easier to manage and potentially reuse apps in other projects.
2. **Centralized Static and Template Files**: For large projects, use centralized directories for static files and templates, and ensure apps have their own directories for custom static files and templates.
3. **Use urls.py in Each App**: Define URL patterns within each app and

include them in the main project's urls.py. This approach keeps routing concerns modular.

Example of Including App URLs

In your main urls.py, include each app's URL configuration:

```python
from django.urls import path, include

urlpatterns = [
    path('blog/', include('blog.urls')),
    path('users/', include('users.urls')),
]
```

10.2 Code Quality and Style

Adhering to coding standards and practices ensures that your code is clean, readable, and maintainable by other developers or future you.

Following PEP 8

PEP 8 is the style guide for Python code. It defines conventions for variable naming, function definitions, class names, imports, and more. Some key PEP 8 recommendations include:

- **Indentation**: Use 4 spaces per indentation level.
- **Line Length**: Limit lines to 79 characters.
- **Imports**: Imports should be on separate lines, grouped in the following order: standard library imports, third-party library imports, and local imports.

Example:

```python
import os
import sys

from django.conf import settings
from myapp.models import Post
```

Linting and Code Formatting Tools

To ensure code quality and consistency, use automated tools like linters and formatters:

- **Flake8**: A linter that checks your code for PEP 8 compliance and potential bugs.

```bash
pip install flake8
flake8 .
```

- **Black**: An opinionated code formatter that automatically formats your code to follow PEP 8.

```bash
pip install black
black .
```

- **isort**: A tool that automatically sorts and groups imports based on PEP

8 standards.

```bash
pip install isort
isort .
```

Writing Clean, Readable Code

- **Use Meaningful Names**: Use descriptive variable, function, and class names that reflect their purpose.
- **Follow DRY Principle**: Avoid repeating code by refactoring common functionality into reusable functions or classes.
- **Modularize Code**: Break down large functions into smaller, focused ones that do one thing well.

Writing Tests

Testing ensures that your code behaves as expected. Follow these best practices when writing tests:

- **Unit Test Each Feature**: Write unit tests for all models, views, and forms to ensure that the core functionality is working.
- **Use Factories for Test Data**: Generate test data using tools like Factory Boy to simplify test setup.
- **Automate Testing**: Use Continuous Integration (CI) tools like Travis CI or GitHub Actions to automatically run tests on every code push.

10.3 Performance Optimization Tips

As your Django project grows, performance optimization becomes essential to ensure your application can handle increased traffic and data loads.

1. Optimize Database Queries

- **Use Select Related and Prefetch Related**: Use select_related for foreign-key relationships and prefetch_related for many-to-many relationships to reduce the number of database queries.
- Example:

```python
posts = Post.objects.select_related('author').all()
```

- **Use Database Indexes**: Add indexes to fields that are frequently queried, such as email or username. Django can automatically create indexes when you define unique=True or db_index=True on a model field.
- **Avoid N+1 Query Problem**: This problem occurs when querying related objects results in many additional queries. Use select_related or prefetch_related to load related data efficiently.

2. Caching

- **View Caching**: Cache entire views using Django's built-in caching mechanisms.

python

```
from django.views.decorators.cache import cache_page

@cache_page(60 * 15)   # Cache for 15 minutes
def my_view(request):
    return render(request, 'mytemplate.html')
```

- **Template Fragment Caching**: Cache specific parts of a template rather than the entire page. This is useful for dynamic content that doesn't change often.

html

```
{% load cache %}
{% cache 500 sidebar %}
    <div class="sidebar"> ... </div>
{% endcache %}
```

- **Low-Level Caching**: Use Django's cache framework to cache arbitrary data, such as API responses or expensive calculations.

python

```
from django.core.cache import cache

data = cache.get('my_data')
if not data:
    data = expensive_function()
    cache.set('my_data', data, timeout=300)
```

3. Use Content Delivery Networks (CDNs)

For static assets like CSS, JavaScript, and images, use a Content Delivery Network (CDN) to distribute them across geographically distributed servers. This reduces the load on your application server and speeds up the delivery of static content to users.

4. Optimize Media File Handling

If your application handles large media files, consider using cloud storage services such as Amazon S3 or Google Cloud Storage for storing and serving media files. These services provide scalability, speed, and security.

10.4 Using Environment Variables

Managing environment-specific configurations like database credentials, secret keys, and API tokens using environment variables is critical for maintaining security and flexibility in different environments (development, staging, production).

Why Use Environment Variables?

- **Security**: Storing sensitive data in environment variables prevents them from being hardcoded in your source code, which might end up in version control.
- **Separation of Concerns**: Environment-specific configurations, like database credentials and API keys, can be managed separately from your codebase.

Setting Up Environment Variables

Use the python-decouple library to manage environment variables in Django:

1. **Install Python Decouple**:

```bash
pip install python-decouple
```

1. **Create a .env File**: Store environment-specific configurations in a .env file.
2. Example .env file:

```makefile
SECRET_KEY=your_secret_key
DEBUG=True
DATABASE_URL=postgres://user:password@localhost:5432/mydatabase
```

1. **Access Environment Variables in Django**:
2. In your settings.py, use decouple.config() to load environment variables:

```python
from decouple import config
```

```
SECRET_KEY = config('SECRET_KEY')
DEBUG = config('DEBUG',
default=False, cast=bool)
```

Managing Multiple Environments

To handle multiple environments (development, staging, production), create separate .env files for each environment. For example:

- **.env.development**: For local development.
- **.env.production**: For production deployment.

Use different configurations in each file, and load the correct .env file depending on the environment you're working in.

Conclusion

In this chapter, we explored best practices and patterns for Django development, including project structure, code quality, performance optimization, and the use of environment variables. By adhering to these best practices, you'll ensure that your Django project is scalable, maintainable, and secure. Following these guidelines will help you and your team build applications that are easier to manage, optimize, and deploy in

Conclusion

Throughout this guide, we've covered essential aspects of building and maintaining a Django project, from the fundamentals of setting up and managing your application to advanced topics such as user authentication, RESTful APIs, and performance optimization. We also explored best practices for project structure, code quality, and the use of environment variables, ensuring your project remains secure, scalable, and maintainable over time.

By following these best practices and leveraging Django's powerful features, you can build robust, high-performance web applications that are easy to maintain and adapt as your project grows. Whether you're working on small-scale projects or large, enterprise-level applications, Django provides the tools, flexibility, and community support needed to succeed in modern web development.

As you continue your Django journey, remember that continuous improvement in code quality, testing, and performance will help you build better applications that are both secure and efficient.

www.ingramcontent.com/pod-product-compliance
Lightning Source LLC
Chambersburg PA
CBHW070423240526
45472CB00020B/1178